FUGITIVE FROM THE CUBICLE POLICE

FUGITIVE FROM THE CUBICLE POLICE

A DILBERT™ BOOK BY SCOTT ADAMS

Andrews and McMeel
A Universal Press Syndicate Company
Kansas City

For Pam and the Cats.

Other Dilbert Books from Andrews and McMeel

Still Pumped from Using the Mouse
ISBN: 0-8362-1026-3

It's Obvious You Won't Survive by Your Wits Alone
ISBN: 0-8362-0415-8

Bring Me the Head of Willy the Mailboy!
ISBN: 0-8362-1779-9

Shave the Whales
ISBN: 0-8362-1740-3

Dogbert's Clues for the Clueless
ISBN: 0-8362-1737-3

Build a Better Life by Stealing Office Supplies
ISBN: 0-8362-1757-8

Always Postpone Meetings with Time-Wasting Morons
ISBN: 0-8362-1758-6

For ordering information, call 1-800-642-6480.

Introduction

I was doing some thinking today. But I didn't enjoy it very much, so I decided to write this introduction instead.

It seems as though every time I turn around, well, I get dizzy. So I stopped doing that. Now I only walk straight forward and backward and it has made my life much simpler. Granted, sometimes I have to tunnel through sheetrock, which is hard on my teeth. And my annoying neighbors are starting to whine about the holes in their houses. And it can take a VERY long time to get where I'm going, given the circumference of the earth and the hassle with immigration.

But when it starts to get me down I remember the story about the tortoise and his hair. If I recall, the tortoise had hair that grew very quickly. For some reason this was a problem. The tortoise eventually triumphed by beating his hair with his flipper.

Now you might say that tortoises (torti to be proper) do not have flippers. But if that's true, how could they fly? Or you might say that torti do indeed have flippers—I'm not really doing a whole lot of research for this part of the book—in which case, shut up.

And this brings me to my main point: I've been spending far too much time alone in my house since I became a cartoonist. My friends told me that the isolation, combined with my newfound prosperity, would have a negative impact on my mental state. So I paid a guy to kill them.

I'm kidding. I don't have friends. At least not good ones.

But if you'd like to be my friend—and Lord knows that's a hot ticket—you can do that by joining Dogbert's New Ruling Class.

As you might already know, when Dogbert conquers the planet and becomes supreme ruler, everyone who subscribes to the free Dilbert Newsletter will form the New Ruling Class and have complete dominion over everyone else. The others (we call them induhviduals) will be our domestic servants. Don't let that happen to you.

The Dilbert newsletter is free and it's published approximately "whenever I feel like it," which is about four times a year. There's an e-mail version and a snail mail version. The e-mail version is better.

E-mail subscription (preferred): write to scottadams@aol.com

Snail mail:

Dilbert Mailing List
c/o United Media
200 Madison Avenue
New York, NY 10016

S.Adams

http://www.unitedmedia.com/comics/dilbert

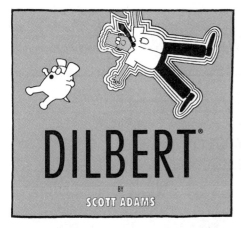

DILBERT®

BY
SCOTT ADAMS

HAVE I TOLD YOU RECENTLY THAT I HAVE A LUCRATIVE JOB OFFER FROM OUR COMPETITOR?

YES

THE PAY IS OBSCENE, THEY WEAR CASUAL CLOTHES AT WORK, AND WEDNESDAY THROUGH FRIDAY IS FREE BEER AND PIZZA.

AS THE NEW GUY I GET TO DATE THE MASSEUSE UNTIL THE COMPANY MATCHES ME WITH AN ATTRACTIVE CO-WORKER.

SOB!!

NEXT WEEK I'LL BE AT MY NEW JOB, REAPING HUGE REWARDS.

WE'RE SO HAPPY FOR YOU.

BUT I'LL STILL HAVE A LITTLE CUBICLE LIKE YOURS.

THE ONLY DIFFERENCE BEING THAT I'LL KEEP A PONY THERE. THAT WAY IT'S CLOSE TO MY OFFICE.

ONE OF MY CO-WORKERS GOT A MUCH BETTER JOB AT ANOTHER COMPANY. I'M FEELING QUITE ENVIOUS.

INSTEAD OF FEELING SAD, YOU SHOULD MAKE A LIST OF ALL THE THINGS YOU HAVE THAT HE DOESN'T.

SO FAR, YOU HAVE A BIRTHMARK, A FEAR OF SPIDERS AND THE LIST ITSELF.

I HAD THE BIRTH-MARK REMOVED.

I'M AWARDING YOU A "RECOGNITION FUZZY" TO COMMEND YOU FOR YOUR GOOD WORK ON THE PROJECT.

DISPLAY IT PROUDLY ON YOUR SHIRT. IT'S GOOD FOR MORALE.

YOU HAVE POCKET LINT ON YOUR SHIRT.

YOUR JEALOUSY IS SO TRANS-PARENT.

... SO I KNEW IT WAS EITHER A LAYER THREE PROTOCOL ERROR OR ELSE IT WAS TIME TO RECALIBRATE THE SCOPE.

HA HA! I'LL AVOID THE OBVIOUS PUN ABOUT D-CHANNEL PACKET ADDRESSING!

I DON'T THINK SHE'S DONE WITH HER KNIFE.

I KNOW. I LOST THREE ENGINEERS THIS WAY.

THANK YOU ALL FOR VOLUNTEERING FOR MY TASK FORCE ON "PALMTOP PERSONAL MULTIMEDIA."

10-7

I'M SURE THAT YOU ALL HAVE A COMMON VISION ABOUT THIS PROJECT...

SPECIFICALLY, YOU THINK IT WILL LOOK GOOD ON YOUR RESUMES WHILE BEING TOO FUTURISTIC TO GENERATE ANY REAL WORK.

MOTHER LODE

© 1993 United Feature Syndicate, Inc.

YOUR ENTIRE STAFF VOLUNTEERED TO WORK ON MY TASK FORCE. NOW I WANT THEM AND THEIR BUDGETS TRANSFERRED TO ME.

WHY WOULD I AGREE TO THAT?

IF YOU DON'T, I'LL TELL EVERYBODY YOU'RE NOT A TEAM PLAYER... SIGN HERE.

10-8

SO... NOW I'M ON THE TEAM, RIGHT?

YEAH... THE LOSING TEAM... BY YOUR-SELF.

© 1993 United Feature Syndicate, Inc.

DOGBERT MEETS THE COMPANY PRESIDENT.

YOU'VE MADE QUITE A NAME FOR YOURSELF IN THE WEEK YOU'VE WORKED HERE.

IT WAS EASY TO GRAB POWER, ONCE I REALIZED THE OTHER EXECUTIVES WERE JUST IMBECILES WITH GOOD HAIR.

10-9

I HOPE YOU DON'T THINK THAT OF ME.

NO, THAT LOOKS LIKE A TOUPEE FROM HERE.

15

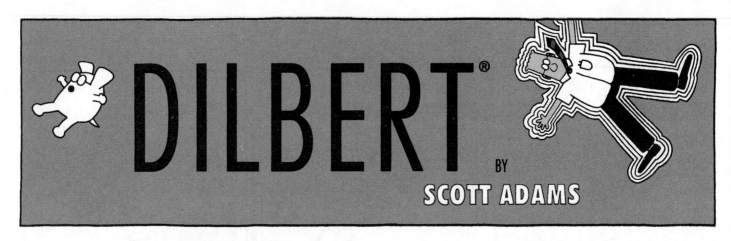

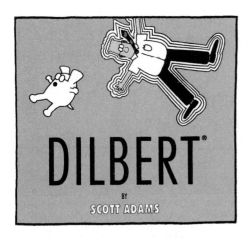

I JUST REALIZED I CAN DOUBLE YOUR WORKLOAD AND THERE'S NOTHING YOU CAN DO ABOUT IT.

YOU'RE LUCKY TO HAVE JOBS IN TODAY'S ECONOMY! YOU'LL GLADLY SACRIFICE YOUR PERSONAL LIVES FOR NO EXTRA PAY!

10-18

BUT AT LEAST OUR HARD WORK WILL LEAD TO PROMOTION OPPORTUNITIES.

YOU'RE SO CUTE. I WISH I HAD A CAMERA RIGHT NOW.

© 1993 United Feature Syndicate, Inc.

ALICE, IT HAS COME TO MY ATTENTION THAT YOU ARE SPENDING TIME WITH YOUR FAMILY AT NIGHT.

THAT'S TIME THAT COULD BE USED PRODUCTIVELY TO DO WORK FOR NO EXTRA PAY.

10-19

DO YOU HAVE A FAMILY?

HMM... THAT WOULD EXPLAIN THE PEOPLE IN MY HOUSE...

© 1993 United Feature Syndicate, Inc.

I CAN'T KEEP WORKING THESE LONG HOURS... I DESERVE A FAMILY LIFE.

ALICE, ALICE, ALICE...

THIS ISN'T THE "ME" GENERATION OF THE EIGHTIES. THIS IS THE "LIFELESS NINETIES." I EXPECT 178 HOURS OF WORK FROM YOU EACH WEEK.

10-20

THERE ARE ONLY... UH, 168 HOURS IN A WEEK.

I EXPECT YOUR FAMILY TO CHIP IN A FEW HOURS.

© 1993 United Feature Syndicate, Inc.

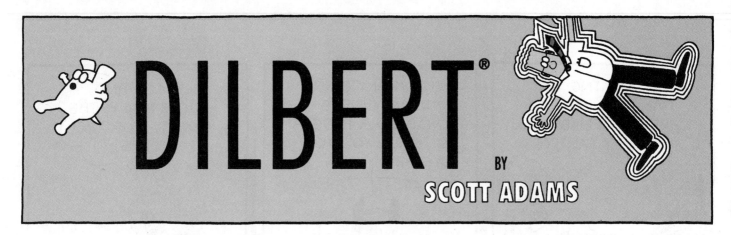

HAVE A NICE NIGHT, DILBERT.

YOU CAN REST EASY KNOWING I'LL BE GUARDING THE BUILDING ALL NIGHT.

TO A CRIMINAL, THIS PLACE MUST LOOK LIKE A BIG OL' SHOPPING MALL.

THE CUBICLES ARE LIKE LITTLE STORES, EACH WITH ITS OWN SELECTION OF QUALITY MERCHANDISE.

IF YOU KNEW WHERE TO LOOK, YOU COULD GET PICTURE FRAMES, POSTAGE STAMPS, CLOCKS, AND EVEN FOOTWEAR.

ODDLY ENOUGH, YOU AND THE JANITOR ARE THE ONLY ONES HERE AT NIGHT, AND YET MY SNACK DRAWER KEEPS GETTING EMPTIED.

10-24

IT'S TOTALLY INEXPLICABLE.

WELL, GOOD NIGHT.

SHALL WE HEAD OVER TO "CHEZ DILBERT"?

LATER... THERE'S A SALE AT "WALLY'S SHOE WORLD."

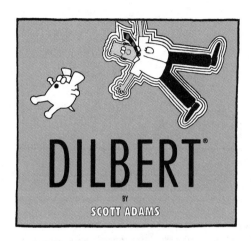

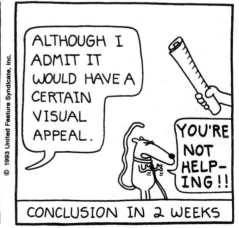

CONCLUSION IN 2 WEEKS

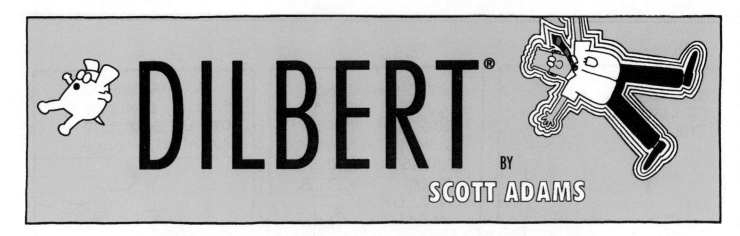

DILBERT®

BY SCOTT ADAMS

IT SAYS THE PRESIDENT CAN NOW RECEIVE ELECTRONIC MAIL.

REALLY?

DEAR MR. PRESIDENT,

I WOULD LIKE TO MAKE A FEW SUGGESTIONS ON HOW TO RUN THE COUNTRY.

AS YOU KNOW, THE CITIZENS ARE MOSTLY IMBECILES.

YOU SHOULD GIVE AN EXECUTIVE ORDER FOR ALL PEOPLE TO MARCH INTO THE SEA.

THEN, THE FEW OF US WHO ARE SMART ENOUGH TO IGNORE YOU CAN DIVIDE UP THEIR STUFF.

THIS MAY SEEM SLIGHTLY IMMORAL, BUT IT'S BETTER THAN HAVING A BUNCH OF UNWANTED PEOPLE CLOGGING UP THE COUNTRY.

AND WE WON'T HAVE TO HEAR YOUR BROTHER SING ANYMORE.

SINCERELY,

ROSS PEROT

11-7

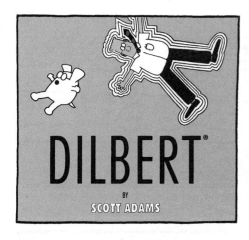

31

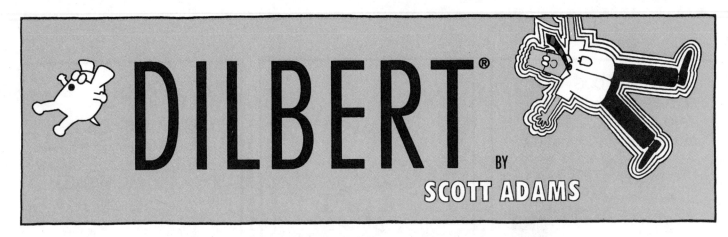

DILBERT, I WANT YOU TO MANAGE WALLY'S PROJECT WHILE HE'S ON VACATION IN ARUBA.

LET THE SHIRK-FEST GAMES BEGIN.

ISN'T THAT THE WEEK WHEN EVERYTHING IS DUE?

COINCIDENCE.

MAYBE YOU COULD CHANGE YOUR PLANS.

NON-REFUND-ABLE TICKETS RIGHT HERE!

THE PROJECT CAN'T BE IMPORTANT IF YOU WON'T CHANGE YOUR PLANS.

HE'S GOOD.

I'LL BE HAPPY TO ADD WALLY'S PROJECT TO THE BOTTOM OF MY PILE AND LET IT FAIL WITH WALLY'S NAME ON IT.

WHEN YOU'RE IN ARUBA, STUDY THE WAITERS CAREFULLY — IT'S PROBABLY YOUR NEW CAREER.

TWO FREE TICKETS TO ARUBA — I WIN.

DILBERT

BY
SCOTT ADAMS

TODAY YOU WILL LEARN HOW TO DEAL WITH PEOPLE WHO HAVE PERSONALITY DEFECTS.

CASE 1: TODD LAUGHS NERVOUSLY AT EVERY ONE OF HIS OWN COMMENTS.

DON'T HOLD IT AGAINST ME! HEE HEE HAW HAW!

REMEDY: TODD MUST BE RELOCATED TO A DISTANT PLANET.

IT SURE IS LONELY! HEE HEE!

CASE 2: ALLEN STARES AT YOU LIKE A ZOMBIE FOR LONG PERIODS BEFORE RESPONDING TO QUESTIONS.

REMEDY: ALLEN MUST BE PAIRED WITH VIRGINIA (CASE 3) WHO FILLS ALL QUIET SPOTS WITH INANE CHATTER.

YAK YAK YAK

CASE 4: MATT SPEAKS SLOWLY ABOUT AMAZING-LY BORING TOPICS.

I... ATE ... A ... PICKLE...

12-12

REMEDY: MATT'S HEAD CAN BE OUTFITTED WITH A READING STAND.

I ... LIKE ... PICKLES...

CASE 5: AN ENGINEER. REMEDY: VERY QUIETLY SEAL HIM IN HIS OWN CUBICLE.

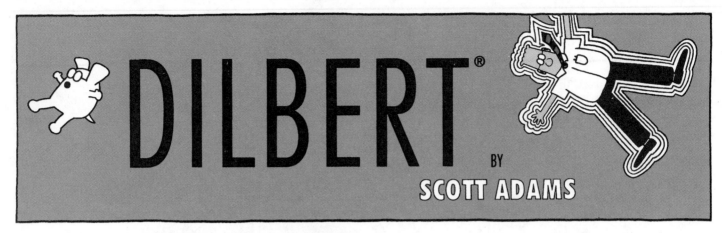

MY TIME MACHINE IS COMPLETE.

I GUESS YOU'LL BE OFF TO EXPLORE EXOTIC AND FASCINATING CIVILIZATIONS.

WHY WOULD ANYBODY WANT TO DO THAT?

BEATS ME.

MY PLAN IS TO SEND ALL OF OUR TRASH TO OURSELVES TWENTY YEARS FROM NOW. WE'LL HAVE MUCH BETTER RECYCLING METHODS BY THEN.

I WONDER WHAT ELEGANT METHODS WE'LL HAVE FOR RECYCLING IN THE FUTURE.

I BET WE'LL HAVE A WAY THAT'S QUICK AND EFFICIENT AND . . .

12-19

UH-OH.

ARE YOU THINKING WHAT I'M THINKING?

PING

WE WOULD SEND IT BACK IN TIME AND WAIT FOR IT TO DECOMPOSE.

I HATE US.

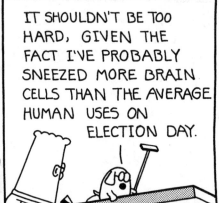

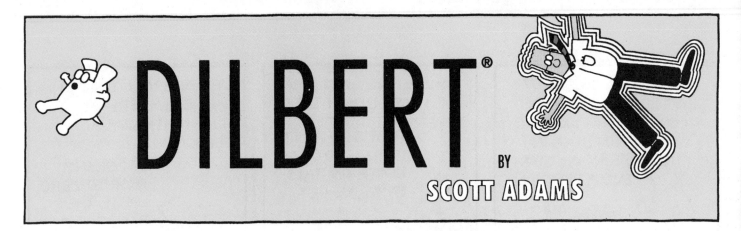

Panel 1: I'M SORRY, DAVE, BUT YOU'RE BEING TRANSFERRED TO MARKETING AND THERE'S NO BUDGET TO TRAIN YOU AS A MARKETER.

Panel 2: SLAP!

1-3-94

Panel 3: WHERE AM I? I NEED A DRINK.

THIS IS A TEMPORARY FIX... BUT YOU'LL FIT IN NOW.

© 1993 United Feature Syndicate, Inc.

Panel 4: WE'VE REDESIGNED THE ORGANIZATION CHART TO SHOW MANAGEMENT AT THE <u>BOTTOM</u> SUPPORTING OUR MOST IMPORTANT EMPLOYEES!

S. Adams

Panel 5: QUESTION: WHY DO THE MOST IMPORTANT EMPLOYEES GET PAID THE LEAST?

© 1993 United Feature Syndicate, Inc.

Panel 6: BECAUSE <u>THEY</u> WOULD NEVER THINK OF IDEAS LIKE THIS UPSIDE-DOWN CHART CONCEPT.

1-4-94

Panel 7: WE'RE FLATTENING THE ORGANIZATION TO ELIMINATE LEVELS AND PUT EVERYBODY IN A WIDE SALARY BAND.

S. Adams

Panel 8: NOW INSTEAD OF NOT GETTING A PROMOTION YOU'LL ONLY NOT GET A RAISE.

1-5-94

© 1993 United Feature Syndicate, Inc.

Panel 9: SO, WHAT JOB TITLE DO WE USE?

YOU'LL ALL BE NAMED BEVERLY.

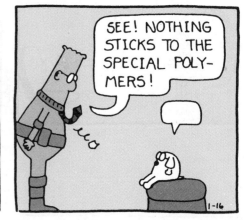

OUR ELBONIAN DIVISION WAS THE LOW BIDDER FOR LAUNCHING FRENCH SATELLITES INTO ORBIT.

I'M PUTTING YOU PERSONALLY IN CHARGE. MAKE SURE THEY USE THE RIGHT TECHNOLOGY.

ELBONIA

OOPS

I HOPE THOSE THINGS AREN'T EXPENSIVE.

THE CORPORATE OFFICE SENT ME TO HEAD UP THE ELBONIAN SATELLITE LAUNCHING PROGRAM.

OOH... BAD TIMING. THE FRENCH DELIVERED THEIR SATELLITE EARLY. WE ALREADY TRIED TO LAUNCH IT WITH THE TOWN SLINGSHOT.

IT DOESN'T GET MUCH WORSE THAN THIS.

IT FLATTENED THE FRENCH EMBASSY. THEY DECLARED WAR AN HOUR AGO.

PROJECT STATUS: WE ACCIDENTALLY DESTROYED THE FRENCH SATELLITE AND ARE NOW AT WAR WITH FRANCE.

MAYBE YOU SHOULD BE A LITTLE MORE UPBEAT IN YOUR REPORT. EMPHASIZE THE POSITIVE.

"... ON A POSITIVE NOTE, OUR HEADCOUNT EXPENSES ARE TRENDING DOWNWARD."

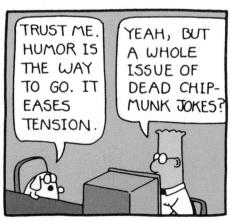

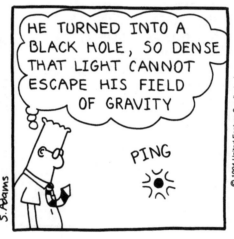

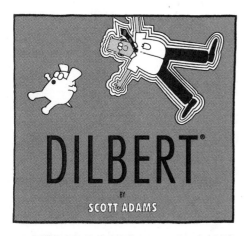

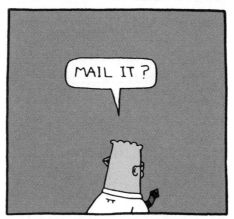
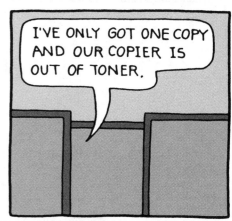

I THOUGHT IT NECESSARY TO PROVIDE DETAILED GUIDELINES TO OUR NEW CASUAL DRESS CODE.

FORBIDDEN CLOTHING INCLUDES: SHORTS, TANK TOPS, TEE SHIRTS, SHIRTS WITH SLOGANS, BLUE JEANS, SNEAKERS, AND SANDALS.

MY MORALE IS SOARING.

APPENDIX "A" IS THE APPROVED UNDERWEAR LIST.

THE NEW DRESS CODE ALLOWS CASUAL CLOTHING ON FRIDAYS.

GULP

YOU'LL HAVE TO MAKE ACTUAL FASHION DECISIONS THAT WILL BE SCRUTINIZED BY HUNDREDS OF YOUR CO-WORKERS!

I'M THINKING "GARANIMALS" FROM "SEARS".

I REALIZE THAT CASUAL DRESS DAY ISN'T EASY FOR YOU ENGINEERS...

BUT YOU'VE EXCEEDED THE BOUNDS OF GOOD TASTE. I'VE GOT TO SEND YOU HOME TO CHANGE.

SHUT UP, WALLY.

I HEARD THEY WERE BACK! I SWEAR!

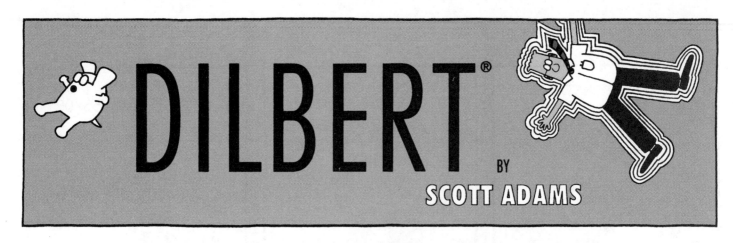

DILBERT

BY SCOTT ADAMS

THAT JOKE WAS NOT FUNNY. YOU'RE INSENSITIVE, DOGBERT.

WELL, HERE WE GO WITH THE "INSENSITIVE DOG BASHING."

IS IT MY FAULT I WAS BORN WITHOUT THE ABILITY TO SENSE THE FEELINGS OF OTHERS ?!

OH, SURE, I WISH I COULD BE LIKE YOU.

SOMEHOW YOU KNOW EXACTLY WHAT IT FEELS LIKE TO BE A DIFFERENT GENDER, RACE, LIFESTYLE OR BODY.

BUT I'M INSENSITIVE. ALL I KNOW IS HOW I FEEL !! AND I'M PROUD OF IT!

BUT YOU'D UNDERSTAND THAT, IF YOU WEREN'T INSENSITIVE ABOUT INSENSITIVITY!!

WHEN YOU PUT IT LIKE THAT, I FEEL KINDA BAD.

WHO CARES ?

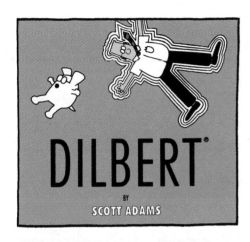

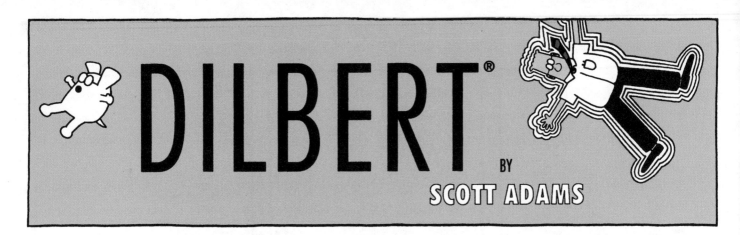

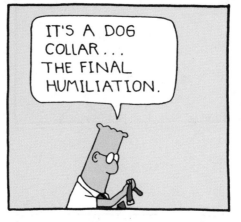

 # DILBERT®

BY
SCOTT ADAMS

DOGBERT'S
BODY LANGUAGE
UPDATE

ARE YOU HAMPERED BY THE LIMITS OF CONVENTIONAL BODY LANGUAGE?

I CAN HELP.

HOW CAN YOU POLITELY TELL SOMEBODY HE'S BABBLING?

BABBLE BABBLE

REMOVE THE OFFENDER'S WATCH WHILE HE BABBLES.

BABBLE

SMASH THE WATCH WITH YOUR DAILY PLANNER.

BABBLE

WHACK!

THIS WON'T STOP THE BABBLE, BUT IT WILL FEEL REAL GOOD FOR A MINUTE.

BABBLE

MMM

USE THIS POSITION TO SIGNAL YOUR SURRENDER TO THE BABBLE.

BABBLE

3-13

NEXT WEEK: THE SELF-HEIMLICH MANUEVER AND THE KEVORKIAN DODGE.

BABBLE

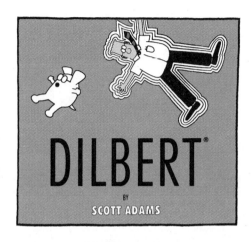

I'VE BECOME A DOOMSDAY PROPHET SO I CAN SCARE GULLIBLE PEOPLE

I'M TELLING EVERYONE THE WORLD WILL END IN YEAR 2000. MY COMPELLING LOGIC IS THAT 2000 IS A BIG ROUND NUMBER.

IT'S B-I-I-I-G AND R-O-O-UND

STOP IT!!!

I'M PREDICTING THAT THE WORLD WILL END IN THE YEAR 2000.

THE CREATOR OF THE UNIVERSE WORKS IN MYSTERIOUS WAYS. BUT HE USES A BASE TEN COUNTING SYSTEM AND LIKES ROUND NUMBERS.

SO YOU REALLY WANT TO AVOID BEING, LET'S SAY, IN MOBILE HOME NUMBER 1,000,000 IN THE YEAR 2000.

I'M FEELING ANXIETY.

THE END OF THE WORLD IS COMING IN YEAR 2000. THEREFORE, YOU SHOULD GIVE ME YOUR MONEY BEFORE IT'S TOO LATE.

IT IS WRITTEN THAT MONEY IS EVIL. I'LL KEEP YOUR MONEY IN DOGBERT'S SPECIAL "EVIL-BE-GONE" DEVICE.

AND IT'S COMPLETELY DEDUCTIBLE ... FROM YOUR SAVINGS.

SO I'M ACTUALLY MAKING MONEY!

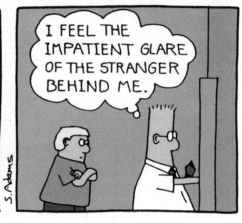

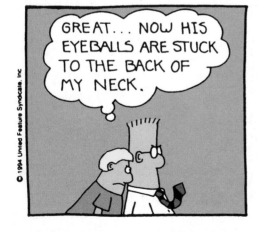

ZIMBU THE MONKEY DESIGNED THREE COMMERCIAL PRODUCTS THIS WEEK! WE'D BETTER FIND OUT HIS SECRET.

3-28

HE'S USING HIS TAIL! HE HAS A NATURAL ADVANTAGE!

I FEEL THE JAWS OF EVOLUTION ON MY THROAT.

GOOD GRAVY! DID YOU SEE HIM CUT AND PASTE?!

© 1994 United Feature Syndicate, Inc.

WELL, WELL, IT LOOKS LIKE ZIMBU HAS DESIGNED ANOTHER COMMERCIALLY VIABLE PRODUCT USING ONLY HIS TAIL.

I COULD HAVE DONE THAT... IF I HADN'T ERASED MY HARD DRIVE WHEN I INSTALLED MY SECURITY SOFTWARE.

3-29

I DON'T PRODUCE MUCH, BUT IT'S VERY SECURE.

HERE'S ANOTHER ONE.

© 1994 United Feature Syndicate, Inc.

ZIMBU, YOU'RE NOT SUPPOSED TO USE YOUR TAIL TO OPERATE THE MOUSE.

IF TAILS WERE A NATURAL ADVANTAGE FOR ENGINEERS THEN EVOLUTION WOULD PROVIDE US ALL WITH TAILS!

3-30

DILBERT, I DON'T BELIEVE YOU'VE MET ROCKY, OUR NEW C PROGRAMMER.

© 1994 United Feature Syndicate, Inc.

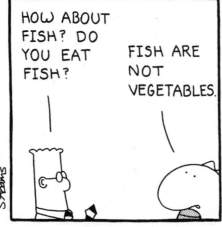

I AGREED TO SHIP PROJECT "DEWDROP" TO SOME CUSTOMERS FOR BETA TESTING.

DIDN'T YOU READ MY TEST REPORT? DEWDROP EXPLODES WHEN YOU PLUG IT IN.

4-14

WE'LL LIMIT THE BETA TRIAL TO FRIENDLY CUSTOMERS.

WE KILLED ALL THE FRIENDLY ONES WITH PROJECT "DUCKY."

YOU'VE GOT TO DELAY THE BETA TRIAL WITH CUSTOMERS UNTIL WE FIGURE OUT WHY IT KEEPS EXPLODING!

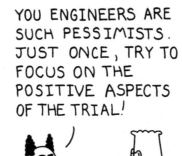

YOU ENGINEERS ARE SUCH PESSIMISTS. JUST ONCE, TRY TO FOCUS ON THE POSITIVE ASPECTS OF THE TRIAL!

WE WON'T NEED TO HASSLE WITH "NON-DISCLOSURE AGREEMENTS."

4-15

I'VE NEVER MINDED PUTTING MAKEUP ON, BUT IT'S A REAL BOTHER TO TAKE IT OFF.

THAT SEEMS LIKE A LOT OF WORK, I MUST ADMIT.

4-16

BUT I STILL THINK IT'S BETTER TO REMOVE THE OLD STUFF.

IT'S ONLY A PROBLEM AT THE BOWL-ING ALLEY.

WE'LL GIVE YOU SIXTY BILLION FOR THE "DOGBERT STATIC NETWORK." HALF OF THAT WILL BE STOCK IN OUR COMPANY.

WHO WOULD WANT STOCK IN A COMPANY THAT WOULD PAY SIXTY BILLION FOR STATIC?

4-21

NOT US. THAT'S THE POINT.

I'D LIKE IT ALL IN MERCURY DIMES.

© 1994 United Feature Syndicate, Inc.

FROM NOW ON YOU'LL BE WORKING FULL TIME ON OUR TAKEOVER OF DSN.

YOU MUST ALSO IDENTIFY ANY UNNECESSARY JOBS THAT CAN BE CUT AFTER THE TAKEOVER.

4-22

THAT WOULD BE THE PEOPLE WHO WORKED ON THE TAKEOVER

OOH, I BROADCASTED THAT MOVE.

© 1994 United Feature Syndicate, Inc.

I PLAN TO USE MY NEW WEALTH TO BUILD AN AMUSEMENT PARK.

DOGBERTLAND WILL HAVE THRILLING RIDES LIKE "THE WEDGIE," AND I'LL HAVE A MAZE IN FRONT OF THE RESTROOMS.

4-23

THE CUSTOMERS WILL HATE THIS.

IF THEY WANT FUN THEY CAN BUILD THEIR OWN PARK.

© 1994 United Feature Syndicate, Inc.

DILBERT®

BY
SCOTT ADAMS

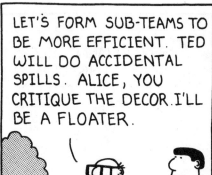

THE DOGBERT CONSULTING COMPANY WILL PLOT A NEW COURSE FOR YOUR BUSINESS.

MY CONSULTANTS ARE SO SMART THAT THEIR BRAINS DON'T FIT IN THEIR HEADS. THEY HAVE TO STRAP THE EXTRA BRAINS TO THEIR TORSOS.

5-9

© 1994 United Feature Syndicate, Inc.

WHY DO I NEED A PIECE OF LIVER STRAPPED TO MY TORSO?

I GOT A LITTLE CARRIED AWAY AT THE PITCH MEETING.

RATBERT THE CONSULTANT

IT TAKES MORE THAN A BRILLIANT ANALYTICAL MIND TO BE A BUSINESS CONSULTANT.

YOU ALSO NEED TO BE ARROGANT AND SOCIALLY DYSFUNCTIONAL.

5-10

S. Adams

© 1994 United Feature Syndicate, Inc.

DOES ANYBODY KNOW WHY A CONSULTANT WAS BROUGHT IN TO DO YOUR THINKING? ANYBODY? ANYBODY?

I'M THE PROJECT LEADER FOR THE DOGBERT CONSULTING COMPANY. YOU SIMPLE EMPLOYEES SHALL DO MY BIDDING.

I'LL BE SENDING YOU ON AN ENDLESS VARIETY OF DATA-GATHERING EXPEDITIONS. THAT WILL KEEP YOU BUSY WHILE I DO THE THINKING.

5-11

S. Adams

© 1994 United Feature Syndicate, Inc.

BY THE WAY, THIS MAY LOOK LIKE A SLAB OF LIVER BUT IT'S AN EXTERNAL BRAIN PACK.

MY CAREER JUST REACHED AN ALL TIME LOW.

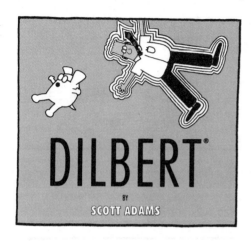

DILBERT® BY SCOTT ADAMS

LET'S SPEND THE NEXT FOUR HOURS REVIEWING THE PROJECT PLAN.

I'VE DETAILED EVERY RESOURCE, TASK AND DEPENDENCY INTO AN EXQUISITELY ACCURATE ROAD MAP.

IT TOOK ME TWO WEEKS, BUT IT'S THE ONLY WAY TO MAKE SURE WE'RE NOT WASTING TIME.

MY TASKS ARE TWO WEEKS LATE BECAUSE I WAS WAITING FOR YOUR INPUT.

AND YOU LEFT OFF ONE TASK, SO ALL THE DEPENDENCIES ARE WRONG.

I'M CHANGING ALL OF MY ESTIMATES TO "TO BE DETERMINED."

CAN WE DO THAT?! I'VE BEEN USING RANDOM NUMBERS.

I'LL HAVE TO REDO THE WHOLE PLAN.

DON'T WORRY. WE WON'T DO ANYTHING UNTIL WE HEAR FROM YOU.

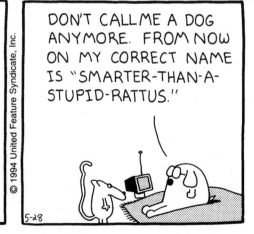

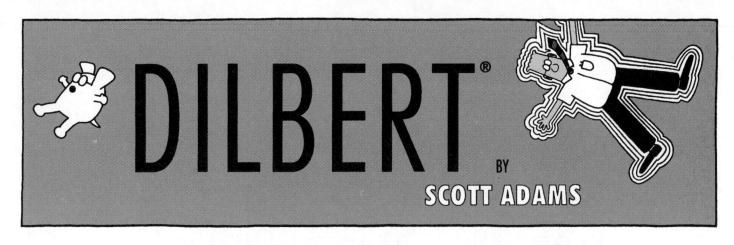

IF I START THE PROJECT TODAY AND WORK NIGHTS AND WEEKENDS IT WILL TAKE ... OH, SIX MONTHS.

IT HAS TO BE DONE IN ONE MONTH SO WE CAN SHOW IT TO OUR VP ON HER ANNUAL VISIT.

6-9

I HAVE TO KNOW; DOES IT EVEN CROSS YOUR MIND TO HANDLE THIS DIFFERENTLY?

I'LL NEED DAILY STATUS REPORTS ON WHY YOU'RE SO BEHIND.

I'VE NEVER SEEN YOU DO ANY REAL WORK AROUND HERE, IRV. HOW DO YOU GET AWAY WITH IT?

I WROTE THE CODE FOR OUR ACCOUNTING SYSTEM BACK IN THE MID-EIGHTIES. IT'S A MILLION LINES OF UNDOCUMENTED SPAGHETTI LOGIC.

6-10

IT'S THE HOLY GRAIL OF TECHNOLOGY!!

YOU BOYS MAY FIND A LITTLE EXTRA IN YOUR ENVELOPES THIS MONTH.

I WISH I WERE SMART LIKE YOU. THEN I'D GET SOME RESPECT.

WE'RE ALL SMART IN DIFFERENT WAYS. YOUR SPECIAL GIFT MAY BE CREATIVITY, A TALENT, OR EVEN THE ABILITY TO LOVE.

6-11

I CAN BURP MY CHEEKS FULL ... URP ✳

I'D GO WITH THAT IF I WERE YOU.

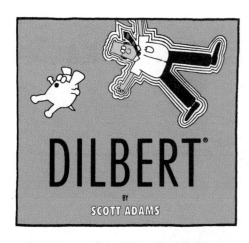

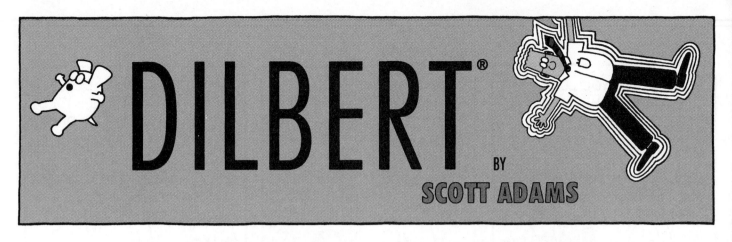

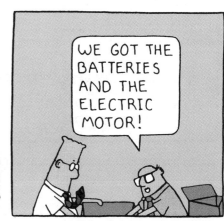

DOGBERT THE PUBLISHER

DEAR TIM, YOUR BOOK DOES NOT MEET OUR CURRENT PUBLISHING NEEDS.

YOUR PLOT WAS LAME AND I HATED YOUR CHARACTERS. AND BY ASSOCIATION I HAVE COME TO HATE YOU TOO.

6/30

FOR SAFETY REASONS, I HIRED AN ILLITERATE PERSON TO RIP UP YOUR MANUSCRIPT. I WOULD USE THE RETURN ENVELOPE YOU PROVIDED BUT I'M AFRAID YOU MIGHT HAVE LICKED THE STAMPS.

I THINK I FOUND A WOMAN WHO LIKES ME, DOGBERT.

NO WAY!

7-1

IT'S PHIL, THE PRINCE OF INSUFFICIENT LIGHT!

HECK JUST FROZE OVER.

THIS IS NOT MY FAULT!

TELL THEM.

THIS WAS OUR THIRD DATE, LIZ. TRADITION DEMANDS THAT YOU KISS ME OR GIVE ME THE "LET'S BE FRIENDS" TALK.

7-2

NO, OUR FIRST DATE ONLY COUNTED AS 85% OF A DATE BECAUSE WE WERE WEARING OUR SWEAT PANTS.

I'M 15% SHORT?!!

IT'S TOO BAD, BECAUSE I REALLY FELT LIKE KISSING.

129

DILBERT®
BY SCOTT ADAMS

WHAT ARE YOU DRAWING, DOGBERT?

I'M CREATING A COMIC BOOK CALLED "THE ADVENTURES OF BORON."

"THE MOST BORING MAN IN THE ENTIRE UNIVERSE."

BORON LOOKS LIKE ME.

GEEZ, WHAT AN EGO YOU HAVE.

IN CHAPTER ONE, BORON SLAYS THE ENTIRE MARKETING DEPARTMENT BY EXPLAINING ASYNCHRONOUS PROTOCOLS.

I THINK IT'S HIGH TIME WE ENGINEERS GOT A LITTLE RESPECT IN THIS SOCIETY!

FURTHERMORE, THERE ARE MANY ADVANTAGES TO ASYNCHRONOUS TRANSFER MODE SWITCH TECHNOLOGY!

7/3

FIRST, THERE'S BANDWIDTH...

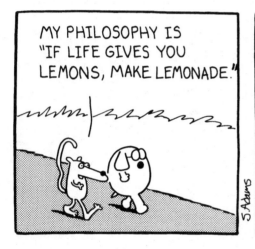

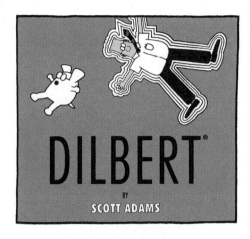

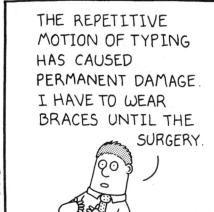

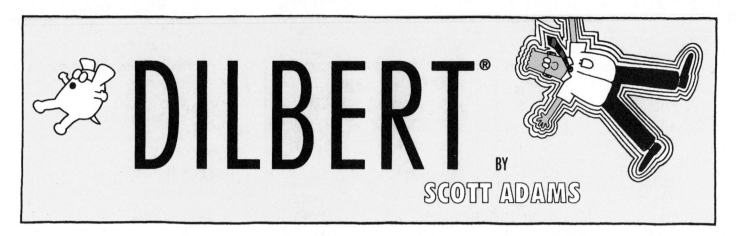

DILBERT

BY SCOTT ADAMS

CAN WE CUT THIS SHORT? I'D LIKE TO GET BACK TO THE INFORMATION SUPERHIGHWAY.

SURE. I'M GLAD WE CONNECTED YOU ALL TO THE INTERNET SO YOU CAN SHARE IDEAS WITH COLLEAGUES.

YEAH, THAT'S RIGHT. I WANT TO GO SHARE IDEAS WITH MY COLLEAGUES.

DO PEOPLE REALLY SHARE IDEAS WITH COLLEAGUES?

IF I GET AN IDEA, I'M NOT SHARING.

I THINK I'LL CHANNEL OVER TO THE INTERNET CHAT AREA AND FLIRT WITH COLLEGE WOMEN.

I'M STILL READING THROUGH FIVE MEGS OF BLONDE JOKES.

7/17

I WONDER IF AL GORE HAS ANY IDEA...

HEY, TIPPER, HERE'S ANOTHER GOOD ONE! HEE HEE!

IT SEEMS ALMOST UNNATURAL FOR ME TO HAVE AN ACTUAL GIRLFRIEND.

WHY?

IT'S LIKE WHEN THE CAPTAIN ON "STAR TREK" FALLS IN LOVE, AND YOU KNOW THE WOMAN WILL DIE IN AN UNLIKELY ACCIDENT.

HEY! WE JUST SAW OUR FIRST SHOOTING STAR!

A HUSH COMES OVER THE CROWD. THIS WOULD BE RATBERT'S MOST DIFFICULT DIVE.

I GIVE IT A TWO.

THE JUDGES WERE CRUEL. BUT RATBERT CAPTURED THE HEARTS OF THE AUDIENCE. ENDORSEMENTS WOULD FOLLOW.

FROM NOW ON, TWENTY PERCENT OF YOUR PAY WILL DEPEND ON THE COMPANY MEETING ITS SALES TARGETS.

IN EFFECT, WE'LL CUT YOUR PAY AND TELL YOU IT'S YOUR OWN DARN FAULT.

WILL THE SALES TARGET BE BASED ON A COMPLEX FORMULA AND INVOLVE NUMBERS THAT CAN'T BE ACCURATELY MEASURED?

YOU BROKE THE CODE!

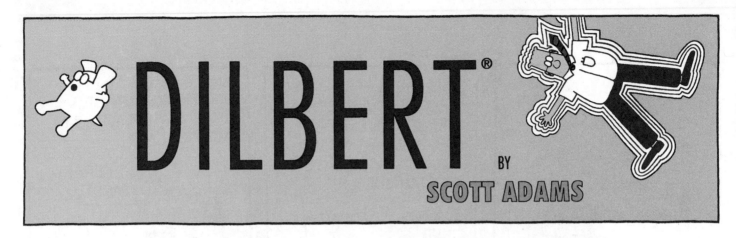

DILBERT®

BY SCOTT ADAMS

"FRIENDS" EXPLAINED

A VERY SPECIAL "DILBERT"

CLOSE FRIENDS

MAY I BORROW YOUR GUM?

SURE. REACH IN AND TAKE WHAT YOU NEED.

"BUDDIES"

CAN I BORROW YOUR HAMMER?

WHY NOT USE YOUR FOREHEAD AS USUAL?

WORK FRIENDS

SO, HOW'S YOUR WIFE?

DEAD. SAME AS LAST WEEK.

BOYFRIEND/GIRLFRIEND (STEREOTYPICAL VIEW)

LOVE.

LUST.

8-14

BOYFRIEND/GIRLFRIEND (MODERN CORRECT VIEW)

LUST.

TELEVISION.

PLATONIC FRIENDS

TELEVISION?

LUST.

MAN'S BEST FRIEND

BY MY ESTIMATE THERE ARE 2.6 BILLION FEMALES WHO DO NOT DESIRE YOU.

NAME THEM.

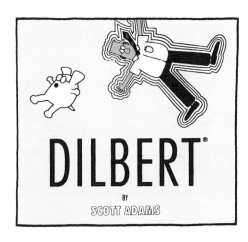

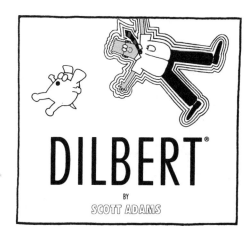

DILBERT®

BY
SCOTT ADAMS

COPY ROOM

STOP RIGHT THERE!

IT'S PHIL, THE PRINCE OF INSUFFICIENT LIGHT!

WHAT'S IN YOUR HANDS?

I'M JUST BORROWING SOME PAPER FOR THE LASER PRINTER. THERE'S NO LAW AGAINST THAT!

I THINK WE BOTH KNOW THAT THE COPIER PAPER AND THE PRINTER PAPER ARE PURCHASED AND TRACKED SEPARATELY.

YOU'VE MADE A MOCKERY OF THE SYSTEM! I DARN YOU TO HECK!

YOUR PUNISHMENT IS TO SIT AT THE SECRETARY'S CUBICLE AND ENDURE THE STALE WIT OF YOUR CO-WORKERS.

HEY, WENDY, THERE'S SOMETHING DIFFERENT ABOUT YOU TODAY!

DILBERT
BY SCOTT ADAMS

REMEMBER, IT'S NOT A PYRAMID SCAM, IT'S A MARKETING BREAKTHROUGH.

THE BEAUTY OF IT IS A NEW RECRUIT IS BORN EVERY MINUTE.

ARE WE GUARANTEED TO BECOME AMAZINGLY WEALTHY?

WHILE BEING OUR OWN BOSS?

YES, UNLESS YOU'RE LAZY OR ETHICAL.

EACH PERSON YOU RECRUIT PAYS YOU ONE THOUSAND DOLLARS THE RECRUITS GET THEIR OWN RECRUITS AND CHARGE THEM TWO THOUSAND, AND SO ON.

EVENTUALLY, EVERY PERSON ON EARTH WILL BE GIVING YOU MONEY. AND THAT ADDS UP.

YOU CAN'T ARGUE WITH THE MATH.

I FEEL LIKE WE'RE A BIG FAMILY.

THE BEST PART IS THAT EVERY PERSON ON EARTH WILL GET RICH!

ACTUALLY, THE LAST RECRUIT KINDA GETS IT IN THE SHORTS.

DILBERT

BY SCOTT ADAMS

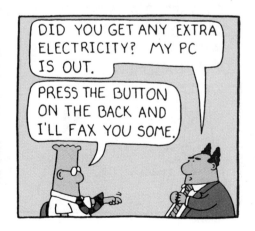

OUR NEW STRATEGY IS TO MAKE DEFECTIVE PRODUCTS AND CHARGE FOR TECHNICAL SUPPORT.

HEH-HEH... OUR USER MANUAL IS TOTALLY INCOMPREHENSIBLE. WE DIDN'T PLAN IT THAT WAY— WE WERE LUCKY.

I'M SO PROUD TO BE HERE.

IT ALL CAME TOGETHER WHEN I REALIZED I HATE OUR CUSTOMERS.

WE COULD DESIGN THE PRODUCT WITH A SIMPLE POINT-AND-CLICK INTERFACE...

OR WE COULD REQUIRE THE USER TO CHOOSE AMONG THOUSANDS OF POORLY DOCUMENTED COMMANDS, EACH OF WHICH MUST BE TYPED EXACTLY RIGHT ON THE FIRST TRY.

BEAR IN MIND, WE'LL NEVER MEET A CUSTOMER OURSELVES.

MAKE IT SO THEY HAVE TO REBOOT AFTER EVERY TYPO.

WALLY? I THOUGHT YOU GOT FIRED.

I DID.

BUT PEOPLE OUTSIDE THE COMPANY APPEAR SMARTER. SO THEY HIRED ME BACK AS A CONSULTANT FOR WAY MORE MONEY.

DID YOU UNDERSTAND THAT? DON'T FEEL EMBARRASSED TO ASK FOR HELP ON THE HARD STUFF.

DILBERT

BY
SCOTT ADAMS

DOGBERT! COME HERE! I'VE DONE IT!

I CREATED A MATHEMATICAL PROOF OF THE EXISTENCE OF GOD!

GIVE IT TO ME.

THIS IS A JOB FOR THE WORLD'S SMARTEST GARBAGE MAN.

WHAT CAN I DO FOR YOU, DOGBERT?

CHECK THIS MATH.

CLEVER... BUT HE TRANSPOSED SOME VARIABLES. THIS PROVES THE EXISTENCE OF HIS DOG.

10-2

NOW WE KNOW YOU EXIST. AND I MUST EXIST BECAUSE "I THINK, THERE-FOR I AM."

BUT SINCE DILBERT WASN'T THINKING WHEN HE MADE THIS ERROR, THERE'S NO PROOF THAT HE EXISTS.

HEY!

DID YOU JUST HEAR SOMETHING, DOGBERT?

THERE'S NO WAY TO BE SURE.

IN ADDITION TO MY CURRENT DUTIES, I'LL BE MANAGING THE MARKETING GROUP.

THE MARKETING JOB OPENED BECAUSE THE PREVIOUS MANAGER GOT RUN DOWN IN THE PARKING LOT.

WHEN THEY NEEDED A GOOD MANAGER, THEY KNEW WHERE TO LOOK.

UNDER YOUR BUMPER?

I'VE NEVER MANAGED MARKETING PEOPLE BEFORE. BUT A GOOD MANAGER CAN MANAGE ANYTHING.

SO... I ORDER YOU TO GO DO MARKETING THINGS... LIKE SEGMENTING AND FOCUS GROUPS...

AND KEEP ON FOCUSING AND SEGMENTING UNTIL WE DOMINATE THE INDUSTRY!!!

WELL, I'M MOTIVATED.

TWO PEOPLE IN A FOCUS GROUP LOVED OUR PRODUCT. SO WE'RE DOUBLING OUR PRODUCTION.

THE OPINIONS OF TWO PEOPLE ARE NOT STATISTICALLY USEFUL...

...ESPECIALLY IF YOU'RE ONE OF THE TWO PEOPLE.

I KNEW THOSE FREE SANDWICHES WERE TOO GOOD TO BE TRUE.

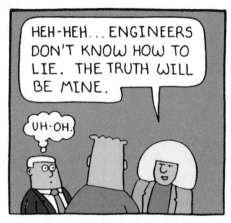

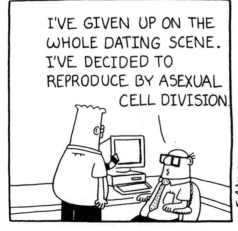

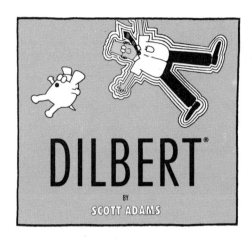

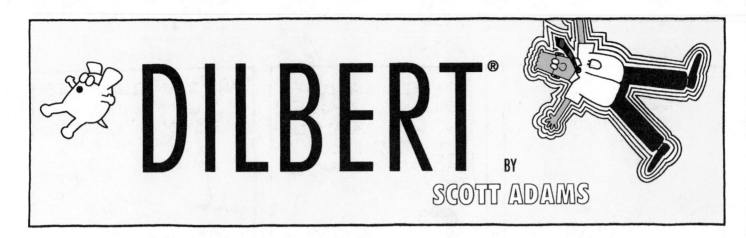

THE COMPANY HIRED AN ETHICS EXPERT TO HELP US THROUGH THE GRAY AREAS.

YOUR CALLS TO THE ETHICS OFFICE ARE COMPLETELY CONFIDENTIAL.

THANKS FOR SHARING THAT. I OWN YOU NOW, WEASEL-BOY.

I HAVE A QUESTION FOR THE ETHICS OFFICE.

IF MY CO-WORKER HAS A "PENTIUM" PC AND I HAVE A 386, IS IT OKAY TO RUN OVER HIS FOOT IN THE PARKING LOT?

IT SEEMED LIKE A LONG-SHOT WHEN I ASKED.

DOGBERT: ETHICS ADVISOR

WE KNOW OUR PRODUCTS ARE KILLING PEOPLE, BUT WE'RE CLAIMING THE STUDIES ARE FLAWED.

WE'RE PLANNING TO FOCUS OUR ADVERTISING ON THE YOUTH MARKET IN POOR URBAN AREAS.

SO, GIVEN ALL THAT, IS IT OKAY FOR ME TO STEAL OFFICE SUPPLIES?

I'D HAVE TO SAY YES.

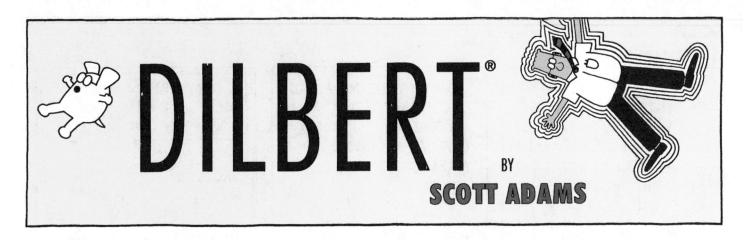

I GOT YOUR PROJECT APPROVED BY OUR PRESIDENT!

BUT HE GAVE YOUR BUDGET TO ANOTHER PROJECT.

IT'S PRETTY MUCH DOOMED FROM THE GET-GO.

BUT I HYPED IT UP AT THE EXECUTIVE MEETING SO SOMEBODY ELSE WILL TRY TO TAKE IT OVER.

STEP ASIDE, FOOLS! THIS PROJECT BELONGS TO MARKETING NOW!

OH, PLEASE DON'T TAKE OUR PROJECT.

YES!

SLAP!

DO YOU EVER WORRY THAT YOU'RE FINDING JOY IN THE WRONG PLACES?

NOPE.

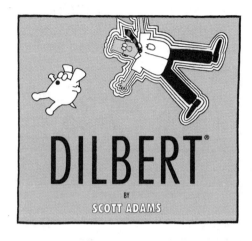

DILBERT®

BY **SCOTT ADAMS**

LET'S GO AROUND THE TABLE AND SHARE OUR ACCOMPLISHMENTS.

I CREATED A DOCUMENT THIS WEEK.

BUT THIS IS NO ORDINARY DOCUMENT!

I BOUGHT A $500 DESKTOP PUBLISHING PROGRAM AND TOOK A TWO-DAY CLASS TO LEARN IT.

I INCORPORATED DIGITIZED PHOTOS AND COLOR HIGHLIGHTS IN A MULTI-COLUMN PAGE LAYOUT!

CLIP-ART ICONS ARE SPRINKLED LIBERALLY AROUND THE PAGE TO FORM A VISUAL MOSAIC!

NEXT WEEK — GOD WILLING — I'LL ADD A TOPIC AND SOME CONTENT.

DO YOU REMEMBER WHEN I SAID YOU SHOULD ENJOY YOUR WORK? I DIDN'T MEAN IT.

OOH.

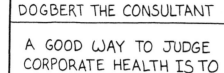

DOGBERT THE CONSULTANT

A GOOD WAY TO JUDGE CORPORATE HEALTH IS TO LOOK AT YOUR EMPLOYEE TURNOVER RATE.

OUR TURNOVER RATE IS VERY LOW. WE ONLY HIRE PEOPLE WHO AREN'T SKILLED ENOUGH TO WORK ANYPLACE ELSE.

MAYBE METRICS AREN'T THE WAY TO GO HERE.

NO METRIC HAS BEATEN ME YET!!

DOGBERT THE CONSULTANT

YOU CAN GAUGE YOUR SUCCESS BY THE NUMBER OF REPEAT CUSTOMERS YOU HAVE.

I'M PROUD TO SAY THAT VIRTUALLY EVERY CUSTOMER GETS ANOTHER UNIT WITHIN THREE MONTHS OF BUYING THE FIRST ONE!

WHAT IF YOU DON'T COUNT WARRANTY REPLACE-MENTS?

OOH... THEN WE DON'T LOOK SO GOOD.

I JUST LOST THE SUBTLE MENTAL CONNECTION BETWEEN MY PERFORM-ANCE AND MY SALARY.

I GET PAID THE SAME NO MATTER WHAT I DO. I CAN STAND HERE AND FLICK MY FINGERS AND STILL GET PAID.

FLICK FLICK FLICK

DO YOU REALIZE WHAT THIS MEANS??!

HEY! YOU'RE GETTING PAID FOR THAT!

FLICK FLICK

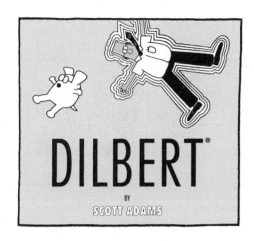

HERE'S THE BASIC PLAN FOR GETTING OUR "ISO 9000" CERTIFICATION.

EACH OF YOU WILL CREATE AN INSANELY BORING, POORLY WRITTEN DOCUMENT. I'LL COMBINE THEM INTO ONE BIG HONKIN' BINDER.

I'LL SEND COPIES TO ALL DEPARTMENT HEADS FOR COMMENT. THEY WILL TREAT IT LIKE A DEAD RACCOON AND ROUTE IT TO THE FIRST PASSERBY.

YOUR TARGET MARKET IS THE HIGH INCOME GROUP. THEY'RE THE ONLY ONES WHO CAN AFFORD YOUR PRODUCT.

MORE SPECIFICALLY, THEY MUST BE RICH, TASTELESS AND EASILY AMUSED. I'VE LOCATED A CLUSTER OF THEM TO STUDY.

THAT DOG'S WATCHING US GOLF AGAIN.

THE EMPLOYEE SURVEYS INDICATE SOME DISSATISFACTION IN MY GROUP. THAT AFFECTS MY PAY.

YOU'RE MY GRUMPIEST EMPLOYEE, SO I'M GOING TO FIRE YOU TO BRING UP MY AVERAGE SCORE FOR MORALE.

I THINK I'M GETTING BETTER AT ALL THE TOUCHY-FEELY STUFF.

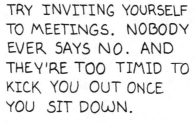

I DIDN'T GET THE JOB IN MARKETING. THEY SAY I HAVE NO EXPERIENCE.

TRY INVITING YOURSELF TO MEETINGS. NOBODY EVER SAYS NO. AND THEY'RE TOO TIMID TO KICK YOU OUT ONCE YOU SIT DOWN.

DOES ANYBODY WANT TO SPLIT A DONUT? I'LL JUST TAKE HALF AND LEAVE THE REST.

SINCE YOU WON'T GO AWAY, I'LL MAKE YOU AN INTERN.

GREAT! WHAT'S AN INTERN?

YOU'LL SPEND YOUR DAY IN A HIGH-TRAFFIC CUBE TRYING TO LOOK BUSY. YOUR MAIN FUNCTION IS TO MAKE THE REST OF US GLAD WE'RE NOT YOU.

HOW DID PEOPLE EVER LOOK BUSY BEFORE COMPUTERS?

EXCUSE ME... I'M ONLY AN INTERN, BUT MAY I MAKE A SUGGESTION?

LET'S FORM MULTI-DISCIPLINARY TASK FORCES TO REENGINEER OUR CORE PROCESSES UNTIL WE'RE A WORLD CLASS ORGANIZATION!

SOUNDS GOOD. GO DO IT.

I'M MORE OF AN IDEA RAT.

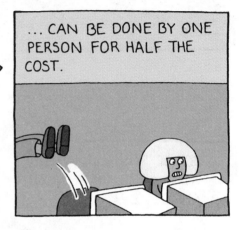

I FINISHED OUR WRITE-UP FOR THE NATIONAL MILLARD BULLRUSH "QUALITY" CONTEST.

IT TOOK TWO WEEKS OF OTHERWISE PRODUCTIVE TIME. AND EVERYTHING BUT OUR ADDRESS IS A LIE.

DO YOU KNOW WHAT IRONY IS?

I SEND MY SHIRTS TO A SERVICE.

HERE'S MY BID TO RUN YOUR TELEMARKETING COMPANY. BASICALLY, IT'S NO COST TO YOU.

MY TELEMARKETERS PAY THEMSELVES. IF THEY GET A FEEBLE-MINDED PERSON ON THE PHONE THEY CHARGE THEM TRIPLE AND POCKET THE DIFFERENCE.

THERE'S NO WAY I CAN LOSE.

DON'T ANSWER YOUR HOME PHONE FOR A FEW WEEKS.

THERE'S A STRANGE SMELL IN THE CUBES.

WE'RE USING AROMA TECH-NOLOGY!

FOR EXAMPLE, RESEARCH SHOWS THAT THE SCENT OF LEMON MAKES EMPLOYEES MORE ALERT.

THAT'S NOT LEMON.

MY JOB'S EASIER WHEN YOU GUYS AREN'T TOO ALERT.

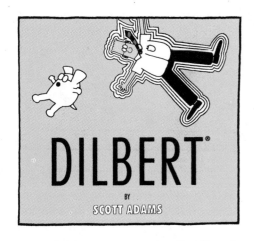

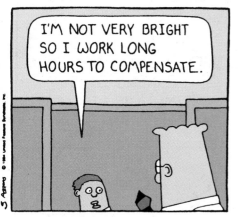

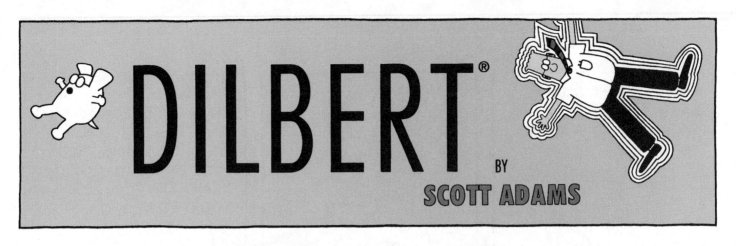

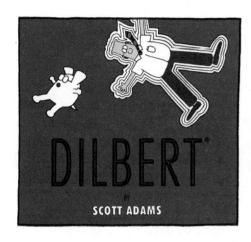

WE'RE TAKING AWAY YOUR INDIVIDUAL CUBICLES. IN THE NEW SYSTEM YOU'LL SIGN UP FOR WHATEVER CUBE IS OPEN THAT DAY.

IT'S BASED ON THE MODEL OF PUBLIC RESTROOMS. BUT I CALL IT "HOTELING" BECAUSE IT INCREASES MY CHANCES OF GETTING TIPS.

EACH CUBICLE WILL HAVE A COMPUTER, A CHAIR, AND A ROLL OF NOTE PAPER ... TAKE ONE AND PASS IT AROUND.

NOW THAT WE DON'T HAVE OUR OWN CUBICLES I HAVE TO KEEP MY BINDERS IN THIS SHOPPING CART.

AND I'VE DEVELOPED A STRONG INTEREST IN GRAFFITI AS A WAY TO EXPRESS MY INDIVIDUALITY.

WELL... IT COULD BE WORSE.

I'M THINKING OF JOINING A GANG.

I'M STARTING MY OWN VENTURE CAPITAL FIRM.

I'M ATTRACTED TO THE CONCEPT OF WATCHING PEOPLE WITH MORONIC IDEAS BEG FOR MONEY.

WILL YOU ACTUALLY FINANCE ANYBODY?

THAT WOULD SORT OF CRIMP THE MIRTH.

DOGBERT, VENTURE CAPITALIST

YOU'LL USE YOUR TECHNICAL EXPERTISE AND I'LL DO THE BUSINESS STUFF. SIGN HERE.

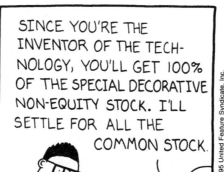

SINCE YOU'RE THE INVENTOR OF THE TECHNOLOGY, YOU'LL GET 100% OF THE SPECIAL DECORATIVE NON-EQUITY STOCK. I'LL SETTLE FOR ALL THE COMMON STOCK.

I HOPE WE CAN AVOID THE TENSION THAT SOME PARTNERS EXPERIENCE.

GIVE ME MY PEN, YOU MISCREANT.

DOGBERT, VENTURE CAPITALIST

MY IDEA IS TO DEVELOP A WORD PROCESSING PROGRAM FOR WINDOWS.

THAT'S AN INTERESTING CONCEPT. I WONDER IF TWENTY DOLLARS WOULD BE ENOUGH.

TO START A SOFTWARE COMPANY?

NO, TO PAY OUR WAITRESS TO BEAT YOU WITH A LOAF OF FRENCH BREAD.

DOGBERT, VENTURE CAPITALIST

I'LL INVEST UP TO FIVE MILLION DOLLARS IF YOU'LL AGREE TO SOME STANDARD CONDITIONS.

I WILL BE CHAIRMAN OF THE BOARD AND OWN 99% OF THE COMPANY. YOU WILL WORK FOR FREE AND WASH MY CAR TWICE A WEEK.

CAN I MOW YOUR LAWN INSTEAD OF WASHING YOUR CAR?

YOU'RE A TOUGH BARGAINER, BUT I PREFER MULTIMEDIA DEVELOPERS FOR MY GARDENING NEEDS.

DILBERT

BY
SCOTT ADAMS

I HAVE AN ETHICAL QUESTION ABOUT TELECOMMUTING, DOGBERT.

DO I OWE MY EMPLOYER EIGHT PRODUCTIVE HOURS, OR DO I ONLY NEED TO MATCH THE TWO PRODUCTIVE HOURS I WOULD HAVE IN THE OFFICE?

WELL, WHEN YOU FACTOR IN HOW YOU'RE SAVING THE PLANET BY NOT DRIVING, YOU ONLY OWE ONE HOUR.

AND THIS MEETING COUNTS.

2/6

DAY TWO OF TELECOMMUTING IS GOING SMOOTHLY. I HAVE ELIMINATED ALL OPTIONAL HABITS OF HYGIENE.

2/7

MY CO-WORKERS ARE A FADING MEMORY. I AM LOSING LANGUAGE SKILLS. I TALK TO MY COMPUTER AND EXPECT ANSWERS.

FOR REASONS THAT ARE UNCLEAR, MY DOG WEARS A GAS MASK AND SHOUTS TARZAN-LIKE PHRASES.

KREEGAH! BUNDALO!

DAY THREE OF TELECOMMUTING: I SPEND THE MORNING THROWING MY PEN IN THE AIR.

POINK

2/8

THE AFTERNOON IS SPENT IN SILENT APPRECIATION OF HOW MUCH BETTER THIS IS THAN BEING IN THE OFFICE.

AHH

ON MY FOURTH DAY OF TELECOMMUTING I REALIZE THAT CLOTHES ARE TOTALLY UNNECESSARY.

SUDDENLY I AM STRUCK BY A QUESTION: WHY DON'T MONKEYS GROW BEARDS?

HEY!

2/9

I CALL A MEETING TO DISCUSS THE ISSUE BUT ATTENDANCE IS LOW.

ISSUE ONE: MONKEY BEARDS.

LET'S GO AROUND THE TABLE AND INTRODUCE OURSELVES.

WHEN YOU CONSIDER THE HOURS I WORK, I MAKE LESS PER HOUR THAN THE JANITOR!

2/10

LOOK WHAT WAS BLOCKING THE PIPES! IT TOOK ME ALL MORNING TO PLUNGE THE RASCAL OUT.

I LOVE MY JOB.

I'M GIVING HIM A RAISE.

I'D LIKE EACH OF YOU TO GIVE ME A CURRENT RÉSUMÉ.

NOW, DON'T BE ALARMED. IT'S JUST SO THE NEW VP CAN GET TO KNOW YOU. IT'S NOT AN OBVIOUS PRELUDE TO MASSIVE STAFF CUTS.

SHOULD I BE WORRIED THAT YOU ALL HAVE A CURRENT RÉSUMÉ ON YOU?

DON'T WORRY. IT'S NOT AN OBVIOUS PRELUDE TO MASSIVE DIS- LOYALTY!

2/11